Quotes O₁

To Live By

"a beautiful mind"

Quotes From A Genius, Autistic, Empath, And Savant

BRIAN MICHAEL GOOD

Brian Michael Good

BRIAN MICHAEL GOOD

Author – Writer – Entrepreneur

A Genius, Autistic, Empath, and Savant

"A book is food for thought… By reading a well written book you will reap pearls of wisdom and have a lifetime of meals."

— Brian Michael Good

I have lived a life buffeted by character-altering hurricanes. My life storms began in a trauma-filled childhood within my dysfunctional family.

My childhood was filled with tension, excessive discipline, and yelling – at home and at grammar school – contributed to a lower self-esteem and academic performance during my formative developmental years. Yelling and corporal punishment instilled fear in me. I carried such sentiments and emotional trauma with me into adulthood. I accepted the abuse that I allowed others to bestow on me. It took me a lifetime to discover that that I was a Genius, Autistic, Empath, and a Savant.

I survived a childhood of verbal, physical, and sexual abuse; dealt with depression, PTSD, the death of two siblings. A bit further on in life, there was the stigma of being homeless not once, but three times, and bankruptcy two times. I was also diagnosed with a six-pound cancerous tumor that was doubling in size every two months. A suicide attempt in 2003 nearly cost me my life. The death of my best friend, divorce, and the rejection of my only daughter was to follow.

Psychics and people of faith say that we all come back, and some of us come back to teach a lesson. The homeless person on the street has sacrificed their life to teach compassion and tolerance to others. The homeless person, if he or she would know this, might ask, why should I try to improve my life if I came back to suffer to teach this lesson?

The answer is that if one is spiritual, the suffering is only part of the lesson. The most important part is to overcome. We must examine our flaws and try to fix them. Then, in the next chapter of our life, we come back to a better existence.

How can one man encounter so many hurricanes, survive them, learn from them, and then strive to make the world around him a better place? This was the question Brian asked himself that led to this book. I have a deep sense of compassion and empathy for others; social virtues that I value most in my life.

What I have learned from my personal experience can give you hope. You are not alone and you are not forgotten. Your life will improve. Peace and happiness are renewed for those who seek it. I believe that you too will find wisdom in the pearls that have washed ashore as a result of my hurricanes and count yourself a survivor.

Author of "Never Surrender Your Soul – your very essence," "RESET: Control, Alt, Delete," and "Quotes of Wisdom to Live By".

Founder of *Nutricare Plus*, *Tattoo You Aftercare*, and the *Best to Live Foundation* is a 501(c) (3) not-for-profit organization.

Nutricare Plus and *Tattoo You AfterCare* markets natural health and healing by offering special formulated skin care products, herbal remedies for the body, mind, and spirit using only the highest quality of herbal, natural, and organic ingredients.

The *Best To Live Foundation* is a 501(c)(3) not-for-profit organization whose goal is to be an outreach initiative providing answers, information, and provide resources for health needs and overall wellness for anyone who needs to survive emotional, mental, or physical stress.

Credits

I dedicate "Quotes Of Wisdom To Live By" to my father, John Joseph Good, and my mother, Mary Elizabeth Good. It was hard for my parents to raise eight children. I love you Mom and Dad…

"Nothing of lasting value is given for free; except for the morals, virtues, and lessons taught by our parents."

– Brian Michael Good

Art/Design: Front Cover, Best to Live, and Big Bang Publishing logos by Alex Polanco

www.AlexPolanco.com

"Perfection on the earthly plain is very rare. Yet, when I gaze upon the artwork for the book 'Never Surrender Your Soul', the Best To Live, and Big Bang Publishing logos, I see Perfection."

– Brian Michael Good

Design: Back by Daniela Owergoor

www.selfpubbookcovers.com/Daniela

10% of the "Never Surrender Your Soul" and "RESET: Control, Alt, Delete" book's profits will be donated to *The Best To Live Foundation*, a 501(c)(3) not-for-profit if an equal amount is match by the donations of others.

www.BestToLive.org/Donate.html

*Take the "**Best To Live Lemon-Aid Challenge**"*

to Help Stop Self-Harm

We need to talk about lemons, in other words, Help Stop Self-Harm. We would like you to take the #B2LLemonAidCHL, as a way to raise money for the *Best to Live* Non-Profit. We challenge you to eat three slices of lemon or donate $10.00 to *Best to Live*. It is our hope that by supporting self-harmers they might eat three slices of lemon and forget why they were about to cut themselves.

Big Bang Publishing

3311 Gulf Breeze Parkway, # 133

Gulf Breeze, Florida 32563

877-502-9166

"Quotes Of Wisdom To Live By" can be purchased for educational, business, sales promotions, youth groups, personal growth, self-help, positive thinking, happiness, motivational, success, inspirational, finding your destiny, self-fulfillment use, mental illness, depression, anxiety, or fear. Inquire about a wholesale price from a distributor or from Big Bang Publisher at the address or phone number above.

Disclaimer

Content and information contained in "Quotes of Wisdom to Live By is not a substitute for professional medical advice, counseling, diagnosis, or treatment. Nor is it intended to replace a consultation with a qualified medical professional. Never delay or disregard seeking professional medical or mental health advice from your physician or other qualified health provider because of something you have read about in "Quotes of Wisdom to Live By" Brian Michael Good, "Author" and Big Bang Publishing do not diagnose, prescribe or treat anyone medically.

"Quotes of Wisdom to Live By" is designed to provide inspiration to reader's world-wide. It is sold with the understanding that the author and publisher are not engaged to render any type of psychological, legal, financial or any other form of professional advice. The content of each chapter is the sole expression and opinion of the author. No warranties or guarantees are expressed or implied by the author. Neither the publisher nor the individual author shall be liable for any physical, psychological, emotional, financial or commercial damages, including, but not limited to, special, incidental, consequential or other damages. The views and rights of the author and publisher are the same: You are responsible for your own choices, actions, and results.

BRIAN MICHAEL GOOD

Table of Contents

BRIAN MICHAEL GOOD

Introduction

Time is in short supply. Recharge your life with over 365 quotes thematically arranged in seventy chapters for daily living to encourage and guide you through difficult and challenging times. "Quotes Of Wisdom To Live By" provides the reader encouragement, comfort, and peace by finding the right words of wisdom at the right time. As you absorb each quote, you will learn that no one can defeat you; you can only defeat yourself. No one can truly save you. You must save yourself.

Learn how to rise from the ashes of defeat by gaining pearls of wisdom and renewed hope. Open yourself to what I have gleamed from my harsh personal experience. You are not alone or forgotten. Your life will improve. Peace and happiness are renewed for those who seek it. In picking up this book, you have shown that you want a fulfilling and happy life.

Reap the manna sown into this motivational and inspirational book. Life's most valuable pearls of wisdom that are nourishment for the body, mind, and soul are found in quotation books. A book of quotes can help change your perspective by allowing you to infuse new activities into your life. Take action, you will be so happy you did!

"Mind over matter, if it matters, you will put your mind to it. The mind is capable of solving anything that matters."

— Brian Michael Good

BRIAN MICHAEL GOOD

Abuse

"A woman's adrenaline can overcome her size disadvantage and defeat a man twice her size, but this surge in strength may not be enough if a weapon is used, unless she is trained in self-defense. A woman's emergency hormone adrenaline effect will allow her to lift a car if a loved one is pinned underneath. The "fight or flight" mechanism spurred by adrenaline for primitive women/mothers allowed them to defend their children while the man was away hunting."

— Brian Michael Good

"Having your car keys in your hand with the ignition key extended between two fingers is much better than holding onto your cell phone, which can easily be knocked out of your hand. If you are assaulted… scream out the word "Fire" not "Rape". People respond better to the word 'fire' because it may affect their safety. If all else fails sexual predators love to be in control. If you grab their privates, they may be startled enough for you to escape."

— Brian Michael Good

"Self-defense should be taught to all children so they can combat rape, sexual abuse, and physical assault, which could happen to anyone. The confidence gained in the ability to defend oneself should never be overlooked in any person's development."

— Brian Michael Good

"Never put your self-esteem in the hands of an abuser… by listening to them."

— Brian Michael Good

"The evil in your life is the abuse you allow others to bestow on you. So, if you are a survivor like me, and others like me, just be fearless. It might be the only way to save you from fear. Fear can consume you and spit you out dead."

— Brian Michael Good

"My childhood was filled with tension, excessive discipline, and yelling – at home and at grammar school – each contributed to a lower self-esteem and academic performance during my formative developmental years. Yelling and corporal punishment instilled fear in me. I carried such sentiments and emotional trauma with me into adulthood."

— Brian Michael Good

"I accepted the abuse that I allowed others to bestow on me. It took me a lifetime to discover that people do not scar or give you pain. It was my acceptance of their mistreatment. I blame myself for not being able to heal from the hurt and the scars that I now realize were self-inflicted. I found that self-pity was one of my greatest weaknesses. Self-pity doesn't do anyone any good. We are all much stronger than we initially think when something bad happens in our life."

— Brian Michael Good

18

"I started by taking an abuse course (not court ordered – my choice – you know – free will). After my suicide attempt I took and passed an anger management course. These self-help programs helped me to become a better person."

— Brian Michael Good

"Children seldom react well to the harsh tone of your voice, by placing your hand over their mouth, by pulling them by their hands, or by spanking them. Positive reinforcement will help your children to develop a positive self-esteem. Positive reinforcement works far better than any form of discipline that causes excessive fear or anxiety in your child's development."

— Brian Michael Good

"Forgiving is not forgetting; it's actually remembering by not becoming an abuser; by using your free will not to hit back with anger, hatred, or revenge. It's an opportunity for a new beginning, a second chance, a learning experience by not allowing anyone to hurt or abuse you again."

— Brian Michael Good

"You must find a way to live even if you suffer from shunning, teasing, gossiping, bullying, shaming, child abuse, sexual abuse, verbal and/or physical abuse. You are the one who is responsible for your own life and the decisions you make."

— Brian Michael Good

"Sorry means nothing if a person takes no future action to avoid being sorry again."

— Brian Michael Good

Acceptance

"Acceptance is letting go of the past to get ahead in the present"

— Brian Michael Good

"Sometimes you meet someone and you can skip forward because of the greeting, the acceptance, and the goodbye"

— Brian Michael Good

"Take responsibility for the decisions that you have made in the past that have bought you to where you are in life."

— Brian Michael Good

"Only you as an individual can improve the way you are viewed. It begins with how you view yourself. You are in control of how you are perceived by others by realizing that your self-esteem should not be connected with the acceptance of others."

— Brian Michael Good

"How you view yourself should be far more important than what others think of you. Accepting yourself the way you are is the best gift you can give yourself. You are much better than you think you are."

— Brian Michael Good

"Everyone needs a chance to be fulfilled with acceptance, which is the impetus to heal old wounds."

— Brian Michael Good

"Waiting was the hardest part, and finally one person and the acceptance among strangers pushed me over the fence totally into the present."

— Brian Michael Good

"Talking to yourself once in a blue moon is acceptable. Arguing with yourself is not acceptable. So, why are you still in denial?"

— Brian Michael Good

"Acceptance and forgiveness will help you heal and sets us free. Say these words and be healed. The past is forgiven. You have the key; just unlock the chain. You are free. It is the only way to be free, find peace and happiness. It is a choice?"

— Brian Michael Good

"Acceptance is a gift that helps you to skip forward and live in the present. Everyone needs a chance to be fulfilled with acceptance which is the impetus to heal old wounds."

— Brian Michael Good

"When you meet another person or when two or more are gathered you will have the opportunity to create the gift of acceptance, the epitome of what humanity should be! The higher you raise yourself in the better treatment of others, the better view you will have of the future."

— Brian Michael Good

"Say hello to a stranger. They will greet you with acceptance and a smile almost every time."

— Brian Michael Good

"Accepting yourself the way you are is the secret to happiness and finding peace in your life. You can allow your experiences to destroy you or redefine you. Forget about whom they are; accept who you are, and who you can be. A choice."

— Brian Michael Good

Ageing

"We are taught to nurture the health of our body, mind, and soul; often they are neglected. While our health declines as each year passes, we value our soul more knowing that it is all that will remain."

— Brian Michael Good

"If you are prepared to enter the afterlife, the day you die should be a bigger celebration than the day you are born."

— Brian Michael Good

"The clock's ticking… The longer you wait to change your life the harder it becomes to implement change. Sixty years old is mid-life if you consider that a healthy person with modern medical care might live to one hundred twenty. So what are you waiting for? Do something with your life."

— Brian Michael Good

Anger

"Rather than listening to the person with anger in their voice, empower yourself by listening to your inner voice of reason."

— Brian Michael Good

"Forgiving is not forgetting; it's actually remembering by not becoming an abuser; yet, using your free will not to hit back with anger or revenge. It's an opportunity for a new beginning, a second chance, a learning experience by not allowing anyone to hurt or abuse you again."

— Brian Michael Good

Anxiety

"Most of us live our lives in the proactive or reactive mode. When you are proactive you tend to be positive and prepare for what could happen. When you are reactive you tend to respond when something is about to happen. A proactive approach can result in a better opportunity for control and fulfillment whereas the reactive mode can result in more stress that can make any problem even more difficult to solve that may lead to failure."

— Brian Michael Good

"When you remember the past too much you don't heal and this can lead to depression. When you try to view the future too much, it can cause anxiety. But when you live in the Now; it makes you feel right; glad to be living in the moment."

— Brian Michael Good

"Just like water, wind, waves, and ice are the agents of erosion of our beaches that bring changes to our shorelines; fear, anxiety, and depression are the agents of erosion of our hope that bring changes to our mental, physical or spiritual health.

— Brian Michael Good

"Fear, anxiety, and depression decreases in exact proportion to your increase in hope."

— Brian Michael Good

"You will not to be held captive by fear, anxiety, or depression."

— Brian Michael Good

"Children seldom react well to the harsh tone of your voice, by placing your hand over their mouth, by pulling them by their hands, or by spanking them. Positive reinforcement will help your children to develop a positive self-esteem. Positive reinforcement works far better than any form of discipline that causes excessive fear or anxiety in your child's development."

— Brian Michael Good

Attitude

"Your attitude affects your self-esteem and how you are viewed by others"

— Brian Michael Good

"Only you can improve the way you view yourself and how you are perceived by others. You can affect change in your self-esteem and improve the way you view yourself with a positive mental attitude."

— Brian Michael Good

"Challenges, hardships, and obstacles are part of what life's journey is all about. You are not always in control of what happens to you, but you are in control how you react to it. You can allow your experiences to destroy you or redefine you."

— Brian Michael Good

"Never let your attitude be the reason for your failure."

— Brian Michael Good

"A positive attitude influences our behavior and dictates a successful approach."

— Brian Michael Good

"I will overcome… are the three most powerful words you can think out loud. Our thoughts often become our reality."

— Brian Michael Good

"No one can defeat you. You can only defeat yourself. No one can truly save you. You can only save yourself. It's a choice."

— Brian Michael Good

"Being more positive can help heal life's disappointments. Your perception of what happens in your life and having realistic expectations creates a positive influence in your life."

— Brian Michael Good

"A person who navigates life's challenges, hardships, and obstacles with stern resolve is able to sail in all winds."

— Brian Michael Good

"Don't be fearful of the future. Own it by allowing yourself to absorb only the positive energy of the people you choose to surround yourself in your new life instead of the negative energy of the old crowd."

— Brian Michael Good

Beauty

"There is more beauty in someone flawed than someone who sees themselves as perfect."

— Brian Michael Good

"If you are independent, strong, weak, confident, intelligent, average, size, shape, old-fashioned, athletic, fashionable, or style less, these attributes or your size, shape, or attire should not diminish your femininity/beauty/essence, nor should your femininity/beauty/essence diminish your equality. I believe in the equalism movement for all humans, absence of required roles, labels, or behaviors that gender may require."

— Brian Michael Good

"You are much better than you think you are and you are more beautiful/handsome than you think you are."

— Brian Michael Good

"Beauty on this earthly plane is often short lived... A beautiful heart and soul will last an eternity."

— Brian Michael Good

Belief

"The most important decision you will make in your life is what you choose for your beliefs since they have everything to do with how you live."

— Brian Michael Good

"I believe that the best defense against – giving up your soul – your very essence – is your choice of a belief system based on faith, hope, knowledge, reason, and logic."

— Brian Michael Good

"Eternal life has just as much to do with what we do right as what we do wrong."

— Brian Michael Good

"Do you believe because you understand, or do you understand because you believe?"

— Brian Michael Good

"Are we that gullible or should we call the story of how Adam and Eve were created as told in "The Book of Genesis" mind control?"

— Brian Michael Good

"Religion is often written with a controlled message, a form of mind control."

— Brian Michael Good

"You should nurture your belief system as a mother nurtures an infant. It is best to choose a belief system that allows you to be fair-minded and even-handed. Be aware you may lose your visa based on the belief system you choose, making your ticket to the afterlife with your soul unable to reach your desired destination."

— Brian Michael Good

"Modern society sets the benchmark for eternal life far lower than it has ever truly been because our morals have lapsed and yet we still want a feel-good comfort about death and the afterlife even though we have morally failed. The moment you feel you are saved, it may put you in a comfort zone where you forfeit your ticket to the afterlife by surrendering your soul with complacency."

— Brian Michael Good

"Eighty percent of the people on our planet have dark skin? If eighty percent of the people on our planet have dark skin and Adam and Eve come from Africa, then I surmise that Adam and Eve had dark skin. I conclude that a dark Adam and Eve were created in Africa, substantiated by logic, science, reason, and faith. That's right Adam and Eve were dark; as dark as my large two inch Café au lait spots birthmark and freckles; remnants of the dark seed."

— Brian Michael Good

"Science has proven with DNA testing that all races have developed from Africa. Darker humans became white when they moved to the northern climates of Europe. They lived in the mountains and ate a different diet than in Africa. Humans in India had a lot of spice and different food in their diet. In Asia, their diet was mostly fish, vegetables, and less meat. Humans adapted to their different environments all over our planet. Aborigines from Australia came from Africa over sixty thousand years ago and they are as dark as the original human seed."

— Brian Michael Good

"One to four percent of the DNA of the extinct Neanderthals and up to five percent Siberian DNA (Asians) is found in the DNA of billions of present day humans except for two villages in Africa who are 100% human. The ancestors of these two villages did not interbreed with Neanderthals or the Siberians. Dark skinned humans have a higher level of melanin in their skin. As dark skinned humans moved out of Africa into northern Europe, they lost the amount of melanin in their skin from the lack of sunlight. Each generation inherited lighter skin. Diet, climate, and the environment influenced the formation of different human races."

— Brian Michael Good

"Adam might need a touch up with darker skin color in the Sistine Chapel ceiling representation of the Christian Bible of Faith's Genesis. It does not make sense that Adam is painted white when eighty percent people living on the planet Earth have dark skin. Again, mind control at its best. It is no longer a white man's world anymore. When it comes to the skin color of humans, it was never the white man's world."

— Brian Michael Good

33

Business

"Seven out of ten people do not enjoy their vocation. Most of the time people find their first couple of jobs by circumstance or chance rather than creating a plan based on their passion. Going to college for four years and getting a degree or working in a trade may increase your income potential an additional four hundred dollars a week more than a person with a high school degree over the course of your career."

— Brian Michael Good

"No human is an island if they want to be successful."

— Brian Michael Good

"Value the passion you have for your life's work more than you value material gain."

— Brian Michael Good

"Great things come from people who are not afraid to risk making others around them feel uncomfortable with their futuristic vision."

— Brian Michael Good

"Authority, control, and wealth come with great responsibility. The Creator expects major shareholders, management and business owners to pay honest wages for an honest day's work. Greed does not give you any reward in the afterlife. You have already taken more than your fair share."

— Brian Michael Good

"If you never venture out of your comfort zone and put your idea into action. Another person surely will."

— Brian Michael Good

"The average woman does eighty percent of the buying, is more intelligent, better at multi-tasking, budgeting, prioritizing than the average man. Forty-two percent of the heads of family households are woman and many of them have a full time job. Women in the USA earn approximately seventy-seven percent of what a man earns for the same jobs. If we change our perception, we may discover that the pendulum should swing to the opposite direction where men earn seventy-seven percent of what women earn.

Now, that's good karma."

— Brian Michael Good

"Individual humans work together with other individual humans but the human race does not work together with nature and the Creator if the human race buys products whose raw materials damage the environment (the Creator's gift) and the wars where humans participate and started/influenced by big business and the wealthy destroy innocent lives."

— Brian Michael Good

Change

"You should effect change when it comes to your emotional, mental, physical, or spiritual health."

— Brian Michael Good

"You must get out of comfort zone if are ever going to change."

— Brian Michael Good

"You can change the future only by implementing change in the present."

— Brian Michael Good

"Without change you will likely fail. If you fail you must change."

— Brian Michael Good

"You must strive to act as the person you would like to become, as an actor would become the persona of the character of a play or movie. It takes at least thirteen weeks before you transition/change into a new person. You must believe that you are the "new you" before other people perceive "you" as this "new you.""

— Brian Michael Good

"The clock's ticking… The longer you wait to change your life the harder it becomes to implement change. Sixty years old is mid-life if you consider that a healthy person with modern medical care might live to one hundred twenty. So what are you waiting for? Do something with your life."

— Brian Michael Good

"It has been said that in a lifetime we live many lives. If you don't like your life begin your next life within your present life by implementing change in the present."

— Brian Michael Good

"Plan a change. Do something different in your life — move out of your comfort zone. What is most important is the foundation, a step by step outline of your plan that will encourage you to do something different outside your comfort zone. Your plan will likely fail without a step by step outline, the change may not happen if you don't plan or follow through with your plan to venture out of your comfort zone."

— Brian Michael Good

Change the World

"Don't wait until the later years of your life to realize that you could've been an integral part of the impetus of change that could have indeed changed the world."

— Brian Michael Good

"If you do not try to change your world, your world will change you."

— Brian Michael Good

"Change your world peacefully or your world will change you. You are either the <u>hammer</u> — writer — supplier — leader — speaker or the <u>nail</u> — reader — consumer — follower — audience. The hammer and the nail were designed to build the world together and create good not to destroy. Become the positive hammer and nail of change that you would like to see in the world. Build a better world."

— Brian Michael Good

"Spirituality will be accepted as the universal standard in our world if the human species is to survive. Spirituality marks a turning point in the world's religious thinking; that the afterlife is open to anyone regardless of his or her religious belief. Unconditional acceptance of religious differences in our society that are derived from cultural differences in our world."

— Brian Michael Good

Compassion

"Have kindness, compassion, and empathy towards others and the natural environment."

— Brian Michael Good

"I have a deep sense of compassion and empathy for others; social virtues that I value most in my life."

— Brian Michael Good

"Without the help of strangers, my recovery from cancer and suicide attempt would have been quite difficult."

— Brian Michael Good

"Help someone in need with kindness including yourself."

— Brian Michael Good

"Psychics and people of faith say that we all come back, and some of us come back to teach a lesson. The homeless person on the street has sacrificed their life to teach compassion and tolerance to others. The homeless person, if he or she would know this, might ask, why should I try to improve my life if I came back to suffer to teach this lesson? The answer is that if one is spiritual, the suffering is only part of the lesson. The most important part is to overcome. We must examine our flaws and try to fix them. Then, in the next chapter of our life, we come back to a better existence."

— Brian Michael Good

Confidence

"Self-defense should be taught to all children so they can combat rape, sexual abuse, and physical assault, which could happen to anyone. The confidence gained in the ability to defend oneself should never be overlooked in any person's development."

— Brian Michael Good

"You are much better than you think you are and you are more beautiful/handsome than you think you are."

— Brian Michael Good

"You are in control of how you are perceived by others by realizing that your self-esteem and confidence should not be connected with the acceptance of others."

— Brian Michael Good

"A person with a positive and confident self-image holds his head up high and is self-aware of their surroundings whereas a person with a low self-esteem or a poor self-image looks away from others or looks down with their head bowed which causes drooping shoulders."

— Brian Michael Good

"Think of a happy thought or something that you are good at that allows you to walk in a confident manner with a smile. Look straight ahead as you walk, make eye contact whenever you talk or pass someone in the school hallways."

— Brian Michael Good

"How you make eye contact with someone reveals a lot about your confidence and self-esteem."

— Brian Michael Good

Control

"All we can really do or control is living in the moment."

— Brian Michael Good

"History is often written with a controlled message, a form of mind control."

— Brian Michael Good

"Find a man/woman/partner that will appreciate everything about you and won't try to change you or control your free will."

— Brian Michael Good

"Change your perspective with less mind control so you can live a hopeful life that creates a path with less fear."

— Brian Michael Good

"A big part of dealing with depression is realizing that you are in control of your own happiness."

— Brian Michael Good

"If you control your body, emotions, and desires, you will be in control of the family finances in your future marriage/relationship."

— Brian Michael Good

"How you manage your expectations is the secret to happiness and finding peace in your life. Peace and happiness are renewed for those who seek it. Take control of your life and be a survivor. Forget about who you were; accept who you are, and who you can be."

— Brian Michael Good

"Most of us live our lives in the proactive, reactive, or passive mode. When you are proactive you tend to be positive and prepare for what could happen. "When you are reactive you tend to respond when something is about to happen. A proactive approach can result in a better opportunity for control and fulfillment whereas the reactive mode can result in more stress that can make any problem even more difficult to solve which may lead to failure. A passive life is as if you never lived at all."

— Brian Michael Good

"Your children are born with free will. You cannot control their free will without consequences. You are meant to be their guides."

— Brian Michael Good

"If you decide to walk the path of life in complete control of your free will you must resist mind control by adopting a knowledge or faith belief system that is aided with logic and facts."

— Brian Michael Good

"Do not attempt to control anyone's free will."

— Brian Michael Good

"If you want to control your lover then do not even think of controlling them. When you do not try to control your partner in a relationship, then you are in control and your partner will always be at your side as your best friend. You will receive far more love and respect than a person who wants control in a relationship."

— Brian Michael Good

"A person whose thoughts are exercised with free will has much more clarity than the thoughts of those who readily accept mind control."

— Brian Michael Good

"Choose to begin to change one day at a time, tiny steps where you position yourself in a steady motion of happiness and tranquility instead of allowing yourself to be hashed around beyond your control."

— Brian Michael Good

"Authority, control, and wealth come with great responsibility. The Creator expects major shareholders, management, and business owners to pay honest wages for an honest day's work. Greed does not give you any reward in the afterlife. You have already taken more than your fair share."

— Brian Michael Good

Coping

\-

Get enough sleep

Go for a walk – Get some sunlight

Develop Friendships

Watch your diet

Change your daily routine

Play some good music and chill for awhile

Exercise, Forgiving, Spirituality

Meditation, Journaling, Limit Setting

Visualization, Goal Setting

\-

"Help someone in need with kindness including yourself."

— Brian Michael Good

\-

"Talking to yourself once in a blue moon is acceptable. Arguing with yourself is not acceptable. So, why are you still in denial?"

— Brian Michael Good

\-

"Songs will never grow old when they are done by great performers. Play some good music and enjoy a comfortable chill by listening to your favorite music. A great coping skill."

— Brian Michael Good

"Develop a way to clear your head… Just say a positive phrase silently or out loud by repeating it to yourself until it clears your head."

— Brian Michael Good

"Find me and you will find yourself."

— Brian Michael Good

"Acceptance: Let go of the past to get ahead in the present."

— Brian Michael Good

"Do not dwell on problems in which you cannot effect any change."

— Brian Michael Good

"Develop a way to clear your head… Just say the words cancel – clear."

— Brian Michael Good

"Everyone deserves a "Me" day without any guilt or regret... Relax and enjoy a day off."

— Brian Michael Good

Courage

"Life's journey often requires great courage to overcome our greatest fears."

— Brian Michael Good

"It takes courage to be able to deal with life's sudden changes. You may not fully recover, but you can adapt. The battle is often won by finding a source of hope that will push you forward."

— Brian Michael Good

Death

"Do not kill emotionally, mentally, physically, or spiritually."

— Brian Michael Good

"Except for my suicide attempt, each time I faced death; I knew I wanted to live."

— Brian Michael Good

"Suicide is often referred to as a permanent solution to a temporary problem."

— Brian Michael Good

"Death by suicide might include any irresponsible, dangerous, or reckless behavior that causes your premature death; except for dangerous situations, someone may encounter in the military, public service, occupation, sports activity, or an unavoidable accident."

— Brian Michael Good

"I am very blessed to be alive and to be a survivor of many near death experiences."

— Brian Michael Good

"Illicit drug abuse, drunk driving, binge drinking, and overdosing on prescription drugs is playing Russian roulette. In each case you knew there was a chance that the shot you were about to take could cause your death.

It was your decision to insert the needle into your body and take the shot of drugs that killed you. It was your choice to shoot shots of alcohol and the binge drinking that lead to your drunk driving death.

It was your decision to take more than the normal dose of prescription drugs or by taking a combination of different drugs without reading the instructions – disclaimers – that caused you die from your drug overdose. Just like it was your decision to place the muzzle against your head and pull the trigger of the gun that shot the bullet that killed you. In each case you took your life and died by suicide."

— Brian Michael Good

"My near death experience from my self-induced drug overdose should have killed me and wiped my brain clean like reformatting a hard drive on your computer. My life and brain were spared?"

— Brian Michael Good

"Why would you kill yourself when there are an infinite number of possible alternatives and positive outcomes?"

— Brian Michael Good

"I ask you from my heart to reconsider killing yourself because I wanted to live when I awoke from my coma of two and one half days?"

— Brian Michael Good

"If you are prepared to enter the afterlife, the day you die should be a bigger celebration than the day you are born."

— Brian Michael Good

"I have no doubt I should be dead from my near-fatal suicide attempt, my cancer, and other times when I was an inch from death. I thought my life would be over when I tried to die by suicide. Little did I know that my life was just beginning? I have everything to live for, yet I should be dead. The Creator works in mysterious ways."

— Brian Michael Good

"I am a survivor. I now respect the gift that The Creator has given all of us: life. I am very grateful to be alive."

— Brian Michael Good

Denial

"Talking to yourself once in a blue moon is acceptable. Arguing with yourself is not acceptable. So, why are you still in denial?"

— Brian Michael Good

"It took this self-induced hurricane; my suicide attempt, when I did not heed the advice given to me to evacuate the coast by properly dealing with personal issues including mental health, eviction, taxes, unemployment, and a failed marriage, which lead to three months of rehab for my twisted foot from my drug overdose, then eight months of homelessness. Ironically, these were the first steps to the road of recovery."

— Brian Michael Good

Depression

"You will not to be held captive by fear, anxiety or depression."

— Brian Michael Good

"A big part of dealing with depression is realizing that you are in control of your own happiness."

— Brian Michael Good

"Some of us will experience some form of mental illness in their lifetime… I rather have depression that can be treated with a pill and my free will to conquer it; than have a physical illness that results in my demise because no matter what I did I could not conquer it."

— Brian Michael Good

"Depression is like a rip tide current that never ends. If you try to swim back to shore, your efforts will be futile and it will only tire you out and make it that much more difficult for you to survive. To escape depression just like the rip tide current you need to swim sideways or seek help; by allowing a lifeguard… 800-273-TALK (8255) or medicine carry you to calmer waters."

— Brian Michael Good

53

"Fear, anxiety, and depression decreases in exact proportion to your increase in hope."

— Brian Michael Good

"We are powerless when the wind, water, waves, and ice are the agents of the erosion of our beaches that brings changes to our shorelines. We have the power to do something when we allow fear, anxiety or depression to be the agents of the erosion of our hope that affects our emotional, mental, physical or spiritual health. A choice."

— Brian Michael Good

"Life is not only precious but living your life in a developed country is a privileged life compared to living your life in a third world country. There is always someone in the world that would be willing to take your place and fight your fight. They will gladly learn to live with your pain, adapt to your depression, overcome your fears; not die by suicide and live the rest of your life at peace. This is why death by suicide is an unforgivable act because there are so many others who would love to have your life."

— Brian Michael Good

"Suicidal thoughts can last for days, weeks, months or even years. I want you to know that you are not alone in your experience. The answers to your questions are all around you. Sometimes, all it takes is to admit to yourself that you need help to effect a positive change when it comes to your mental, physical, emotional or spiritual health. Call 800-273-TALK (8255) if you need a friend to lean on."

— Brian Michael Good

"There will never be enough breath in your lungs to sustain the depths of your despair; just like the depths of the ocean cannot be sustained indefinitely without being resupplied with fresh air. In both cases you will not survive unless you take the necessary action needed before your final breath. Come up for air by going for a walk and just breathe."

— Brian Michael Good

Desire

"Think about a car not having ample petro/gas to start the engine, as the body not getting the proper nutrition, preventing the driver from arriving at their desired destination, an engaged mind likewise cannot develop the knowledge base of life skills that will be needed to achieve upward mobility."

— Brian Michael Good

"Be aware you may lose your visa based on the belief system you choose, making your ticket to the afterlife with your soul unable to reach your desired destination."

— Brian Michael Good

"Guide your children so they can realize their own separate dream. Lead them in the right direction only means guidance, not pushing them against their will into a school, a sport, a high school, a social group, a college, or leading them on a career path where they will lack the passion or desire to excel."

— Brian Michael Good

"If you control your body, emotions, and desires, you will be in control of the finances in your future marriage/relationship."

— Brian Michael Good

Despair

"There will never be enough breath in your lungs to sustain the depths of your despair; just like the depths of the ocean cannot be sustained indefinitely without being resupplied with fresh air. In both cases you will not survive unless you take the necessary action needed before your final breath. Come up for air by going for a walk and just breathe."

— Brian Michael Good

"You can do all the right things and still have bad results. Bad things happen to good people and sometimes bad things happen for a reason. Someday, in your future, there is going to be a better tomorrow. Know that things will get better."

— Brian Michael Good

"How you manage your expectations is the secret to happiness and finding peace in your life. Peace and happiness are renewed for those who seek it. Take control of your life and be a survivor. Forget about who you were; accept who you are, and who you can be."

— Brian Michael Good

"Changes or events that happen in your life can be fixed or healed with a positive mental attitude. A choice. But when your life is over; it never comes back and you'll never know you could have made it to where you once thought was impossible. Again, a choice."

— Brian Michael Good

"Stop feeling sorry for yourself because only you can save yourself. Pick yourself up, go take a walk, meet a new friend, or ask someone out on a date. Meet a new friend that will make you laugh."

— Brian Michael Good

"Do not judge your lot in life and do not over judge yourself. Do not feel sorry for yourself. Stop whining. Do not self-pity. Life can always be worse than it is. Nothing is the end of the world. There is always a way to fix it."

— Brian Michael Good

Destiny and Life

"Six weeks after conception, the nervous system of the developing brain of a fetus is able to send out impulses to control its body functions and movements. Since the lack of brain activity is the accepted as the sign of death in the medical community and accepted by many people of faith. It might be safe to say that the beginning of brain activity is a definitive sign of life.

The heart of a fetus first begins to beat at three weeks, about 18 days after conception. I believe that life begins when the heart of the fetus starts to beat since there has been one medical case where a child was born without a brain and lived for twelve years with a beating heart."

— Brian Michael Good

"Your life can change without notice; in just seconds that could change your life's course forever… only if you let it. Nearly everything can be fixed. A choice."

— Brian Michael Good

"Integrity, Honor, Trust, Loyalty, Respect, Reputation. These values should be nurtured as a mother cares for an infant. Without the proper attention, all of these values can be lost from one careless decision."

— Brian Michael Good

"Sometimes the hand that life has dealt us is because of the decisions and actions we have made. We realize we dealt the hand ourselves."

— Brian Michael Good

"Meeting your destiny doesn't happen without a plan, a plan doesn't happen without a purpose, a purpose doesn't happen without finding your passion, a passion isn't discovered without the pursuit of activities that you enjoy."

— Brian Michael Good

"Never put your destiny in the hands of a naysayer… by listening to them."

— Brian Michael Good

"Finding your destiny has much to do with finding out what makes you happy. You need to take the necessary steps to put your life on the right course to find your passion and achieve your destiny. Choose a passion you enjoy doing; so even if do not meet your destiny you will be happy with your life. Always have a backup plan. You may find that your hobby is the passion that becomes your destiny."

— Brian Michael Good

"The only thing you will truly regret in your life is who you could have been. Life will always be what you make of it. Forget about whom you were; accept who you are, and who you can be."

— Brian Michael Good

"Find a purpose for your life and you will do extraordinary things.

You are in center of your happiness when you pursue your passion.

When you pursue your passion, you are the master of your environment.

When you are the master of your environment you often meet your destiny."

— Brian Michael Good

"Life's experiences are not woven with a constant thread; Life in our world is constantly changing. We must repurpose what we have endured and the lessons we have learned; creating a renewed sense of hope. Life is what it is. The question is… What are you willing to do to change your life?"

— Brian Michael Good

"Mind over matter, if it matters, you will put your mind to it. The mind is capable of solving anything that matters."

— Brian Michael Good

"Tomorrow is full of promise if you prepare for today."

— Brian Michael Good

"Every endeavor in life is not about the odds of success but about your passion, your belief, and your indomitable will."

— Brian Michael Good

"How you play the hand that life has dealt you will define your human spirit. Do not judge your lot in life and do not over judge yourself. Do not feel sorry for yourself. Stop whining and have no self-pity. Nothing is the end of the world. Life can always be worse than it is. There is always a way to fix it."

— Brian Michael Good

"Great things come from people who are not afraid to risk making others around them feel uncomfortable with their futuristic vision."

— Brian Michael Good

"Change your world peacefully or your world will change you. You are either the <u>hammer</u> — writer — supplier — leader — speaker or the <u>nail</u> — reader — consumer — follower — audience. The hammer and the nail were designed to build the world together and create good not to destroy. Become the positive hammer and nail of change that you would like to see in the world. Build a better world."

— Brian Michael Good

"The costs to society are much less to feed an open mind with a school meal than to feed a closed mind that no longer has the appetite to believe in the American Dream."

— Brian Michael Good

"The pursuit of the American Dream is alive but not well and may seem obscure and improbable for most of us since is it is harder than ever to achieve with such an abundance of low paying jobs; but the truth is the American Dream has never been easy to attain. Yet, the elusive American Dream is still achievable for anyone with the right attitude, buying behavior, education, savings, knowing the value of hard work, and indomitable will."

— Brian Michael Good

"Let us not mourn the passing of the American Dream just because we have given up hope; many of us are left hoping to win the lottery. Anyone living near or below the poverty line knows very well that the higher cost of services essential for daily survival is a formidable goal for them. Still, many Americans take these blessings for granted."

— Brian Michael Good

"Perception is 98% of reality. Change your perception and you will change your life.

RESET: You are in: CONTROL Change your perspective: ALT

Forget the past: DELETE

— Brian Michael Good

"Meet your destiny. The contribution of one human's efforts might be the difference between the survival or destruction of humanity."

— Brian Michael Good

Diligence

"Integrity, Honor, Trust, Loyalty, Respect, Reputation. These values should be nurtured as a mother cares for an infant. Without the proper attention, all of these values can be lost from one careless decision."

— Brian Michael Good

"Never look back, never give up, never stop trying, never quit, not even a bit."

— Brian Michael Good

Empathy

"If you suffer from Fear, Anxiety, Anger, or Depression you may be picking up people's feelings and emotions. You might be an <u>Empath</u>."

— Brian Michael Good

"Have kindness, compassion, and empathy towards others and the natural environment."

— Brian Michael Good

"It is nice to be popular but it is popular to be nice."

— Brian Michael Good

"I have a deep sense of compassion and empathy for others; social virtues that I value most in my life."

— Brian Michael Good

Endurance

"Challenges, hardships and obstacles are what life is all about and if you face them with a positive attitude; you will find that it takes half the effort to overcome them. You will find that the sum of your challenges, hardships, and obstacles will define your human spirit and years later as you reflect on your experiences you will realize they have become your strength."

— Brian Michael Good

"A person who navigates life's challenges, hardships and obstacles with stern resolve is able to sail in all winds."

— Brian Michael Good

"You can allow your experiences to destroy you or redefine you. Forget about whom they are; accept who you are, and who you can be. A choice."

— Brian Michael Good

Environment

"Each individual should strive to live in harmony with the eco-system and the natural environment

— Brian Michael Good

"Climate change as the result of the depletion of our forests, the burning of fossil fuels, large-scale industrial air pollution, environmentally destructive mining methods, irresponsible storage and disposal of contaminants that pollute our air, water and soil should concern all of us. Our planet is essentially being terraformed by mankind's greed. If an alien race was to terraform and warm our planet; we would not allow it. So, why are we allowing mankind's destructive nature to make us sick and kill the planet earth, our only home?"

— Brian Michael Good

"The human race will not survive at the current consumption rate of the top twenty developed countries. By the 2030s, there will be very few third world countries, these countries will have stable developed economies, with large populations that will be vying for the same natural resources and food. I cannot stress this enough. As I said before being spiritual includes protecting the natural environment by practicing the 7Rs?"

— Brian Michael Good

"There's more to well-being than living a spiritual life, it's the state of our planet's future. A spiritual person cares about the environment and sustainability. Being spiritual includes protecting the natural environment by practicing the 7R's...

Reduce your carbon footprint.

Rethink, Refuse, Repurpose, and **Reuse** items before you discard.

Recycle items that you discard.

Reclaim hazardous waste properly at an eco-collection facility."

— Brian Michael Good

"Individual humans work together with other individual humans but the human race does not work together with nature and the Creator if the human race buys products whose raw materials damage the environment (the Creator's gift) and the wars where humans participate and started/influenced by big business and the wealthy destroy innocent lives."

— Brian Michael Good

"Make a conscious decision to use products for an additional year or two when they contain raw materials that are dangerous (lithium-ion batteries in our cell phones) to transport, hazardous to dispose of back into the environment or may be harmful to the earth in its initial procurement of its raw materials. Purchase manufacturer refurbished products. They are just as good as new items with many of the parts replaced, and sold at far less cost as new product. If you purchase new, be aware that sustainable products do make an environmental impact worldwide, providing economic benefits while protecting the local eco-system that may affect the habitability on Earth, Gaia, and the health of its inhabitants."

— Brian Michael Good

Failure

"Failures are stepping-stones to success and your destiny. Failure allows you to reinvent yourself."

— Brian Michael Good

"You learn more from your mistakes and failures than from any degree of success. Success can only be grasped for a moment before it becomes a distant oasis not to be found again unless you thirst for the knowledge found in the well fed by your mistakes and failures."

— Brian Michael Good

"We are all human, be comfortable with this fact."

— Brian Michael Good

"Never let your attitude be the reason for your failure."

— Brian Michael Good

"Failures are stepping stones to success and your destiny. Failure allows you to reinvent yourself... Instead of looking at your problems as something that is holding you back. View your problems as a solution you haven't found yet."

— Brian Michael Good

"Most of us live our lives in the proactive, reactive or passive mode. When you are proactive you tend to be positive and prepare for what could happen. "When you are reactive you tend to respond when something is about to happen. A proactive approach can result in a better opportunity for control and fulfillment whereas the reactive mode can result in more stress that can make any problem even more difficult to solve which may lead to failure. A passive life is as if you never lived at all."

— Brian Michael Good

"Sometimes failure or defeat is not an option. You can allow your experiences to destroy you or redefine you. No one can defeat you. You can only defeat yourself."

— Brian Michael Good

"Plan a change. Do something different in your life — move out of your comfort zone. What is most important is the foundation, a step by step outline of your plan that will encourage you to do something different outside your comfort zone. Your plan will likely fail without a step by step outline, the change may not happen if you don't plan or follow through with your plan to venture out of your comfort zone."

— Brian Michael Good

"No success is ever met without a series of failures."

— Brian Michael Good

Faithfulness

"True faithfulness is often found in the enduring patience of your partner, listening to your long-winded conversations."

— Brian Michael Good

"Trust, faithfulness, and loyalty should define your relationships."

— Brian Michael Good

Family

"Reading a story at bedtime is still a great way for parents to teach their child the lessons necessary for positive social development. If you read stories to your children with morals and virtues until the age of reasoning, they will learn many important life lessons that will help reinforce good behavior as they mature."

— Brian Michael Good

"Children learn more from your actions, and behavior than any lessons obtained from a book or any advice you may give them."

— Brian Michael Good

"Children are not always mature enough to follow advice but often learn from the example of others."

— Brian Michael Good

"Children seldom react well to the harsh tone of your voice, by placing your hand over their mouth, by pulling them by their hands, or by spanking them. Positive reinforcement will help your children to develop a positive self-esteem. Positive reinforcement works far better than any form of discipline that causes excessive fear or anxiety in your child's development."

— Brian Michael Good

"Your children are born with free will. You cannot control their free will without consequences. You are meant to be their guides."

— Brian Michael Good

"Obey your parents, move out and you will find out life could be much harder. You will find that living on the streets and doing whatever it takes to survive will be much harder than living with your parents. Move out only if you might kill yourself or if you are being abused."

— Brian Michael Good

"If you control your body, emotions, and desires, you will be in control of the family finances in your future marriage/relationship."

— Brian Michael Good

"In any good marriage, a woman's voice is equal to man's voice. The same should be true in our open society. Yes, women count as much as men. They count even more than men do, if you consider that women can do what men have considered to be "their domain" of feats, work, sports, business accomplishments, and bear children. You have to admit Women are equal to men."

— Brian Michael Good

"You may choose to be a mother or father someday. However, you will have to earn your acceptance as a good role model and gain respect from your child every day. Acceptance from our children can no longer be taken for granted in any society."

— Brian Michael Good

"Try not to make my mistake (rejection of my daughter); the best thing you can achieve in life is raising a good human by being in their life every day. Children and teenagers need both parents. I wish I had taken some kind of parent training but I guess you have to walk the right path."

— Brian Michael Good

"Take responsibility for any action or reaction you have with your children. Once, my daughter jumped on me with such enthusiasm and embrace when I was about to have a bowl of soup that I placed on the wooden arm of the sofa. I blew the call, when my daughter jumped on me, with all love for her father when she made this innocent, enthusiastic jump of joy. The bowl of soup spilled all over the floor; I said to her, "Why did you make the soup spill?"

"The soup made a mess of the floor and rug. I was the one responsible because I put the soup bowl on the arm of the sofa. Little did I realize that at nine years old it was the last time she would embrace me with such enthusiasm of her love for me. Remember, if the soup spills on the floor next time it will be my fault entirely, never again your fault."

— Brian Michael Good

"Nothing of lasting value is given for free; except for the morals, virtues, and lessons taught by our parents."

— Brian Michael Good

Fear

"You will not to be held captive by fear, anxiety or depression."

— Brian Michael Good

"Fear decreases in exact proportion to your increase in hope."

— Brian Michael Good

"You are chained by your decision to accept the fear, scars, and pain that you allowed others to bestow on you. It was your acceptance of their mistreatment that stops you from being able to heal from all the attacks. You have the key once you discover that the fear, scars, and pain were self-inflected. Just unlock your chains. A choice."

— Brian Michael Good

"You have only your own perception of reality to fear. If you don't like it... Change it... We all have the power to do something. You have free will."

— Brian Michael Good

"Some of us compromise with their fear, some of us adapt to their fear, some of us are consumed by their fear, some of us are defeated by their fear, and some of us overcome their fear. Confronting fear is an instinctive response for survival. To be held captive by fear in any form is always a choice."

— Brian Michael Good

"Fear is a choice. Feeling paralyzed with fear is not an option. Just be fearless. It might be your only way to save yourself from fear. Fear can consume you and spit you out dead."

— Brian Michael Good

"Fear not. Never look back, never give up, never stop trying, never quit, not even a bit."

— Brian Michael Good

"Life's journey often requires great courage to overcome our greatest fears."

— Brian Michael Good

"Don't be fearful of the future. Own it by allowing yourself to absorb only the positive energy of the people you choose to surround yourself in your new life instead of the negative energy of the old crowd."

— Brian Michael Good

"The evil in your life is the abuse you allow others to bestow on you. So, if you are a survivor like me and others like me, just be fearless. It might be your only way to save yourself from fear. Fear can consume you and spit you out dead."

— Brian Michael Good

"You can't stay in the nest your whole life; you must leave your comfort zone, spread your wings, and learn to fly on your own."

— Brian Michael Good

Friendship

"Stop feeling sorry for yourself because only you can save yourself. Pick yourself up, go take a walk, meet a new friend or ask someone out on a date. Meet a new friend that will make you laugh."

— Brian Michael Good

"You never know who your friends are. It could be your wife and you better make her your best friend because she knows you like a book and you are well read by her."

— Brian Michael Good

"When you graduate high school or college, you may have made your last friend except if you have the opportunity to make a friend at work or with your partner. But you always have yourself."

— Brian Michael Good

"Develop new friendships; it may be the reason you live."

— Brian Michael Good

"If you want to be respected, try listening to others first. You will make friends and be loved."

— Brian Michael Good

"A person who chooses luxuries as prudently as they should choose their friendships will have a greater opportunity to be rewarded in the afterlife."

— Brian Michael Good

"Try not to create your own loneliness by staying with the old you by not having an awakening. Acceptance is a gift and you get more acceptance than you give. Try to listen first, be more quiet and at peace. You will discover that people will call you, they will invite your friendship, and you will be loved."

— Brian Michael Good

Forgiveness

"When you forgive… You will have made the decision to move forward. Only you can heal yourself. It is a choice."

— Brian Michael Good

"Start a new journey filled with the passion and the love and forgiveness that you deserve."

— Brian Michael Good

"Trust, faithfulness, and loyalty should define your relationships."

— Brian Michael Good

"Forgiveness removes fear. Forgiving others who have hurt you will help you heal. How you view your life will help you to survive."

— Brian Michael Good

"Forgiving is not forgetting; it's actually remembering by not becoming an abuser; yet, using your free will not to hit back with anger or revenge. It's an opportunity for a new beginning, a second chance, a learning experience by not allowing anyone to hurt or abuse you again."

— Brian Michael Good

Free Will

"Free will allows us to paint the canvas of how we choose to live our lives."

— Brian Michael Good

"We are born with free will, a soul, and a ticket to the afterlife. Decide to keep your ticket to the afterlife by never surrendering your soul. Count yourself a survivor."

— Brian Michael Good

"Free will is our greatest gift after life itself, that being said, Free will must be exercised wisely. As much as is humanly possible."

— Brian Michael Good

"Do not attempt to control anyone's free will."

— Brian Michael Good

"We can choose to steer off course or amend it. We have choices. You have free will."

— Brian Michael Good

"If you decide to walk the path of life in complete control of your free will you must resist mind control by adopting a knowledge or faith belief system that is aided with logic and facts."

— Brian Michael Good

"A person whose thoughts are exercised with free will has much more clarity than the thoughts of those who readily accept mind control."

— Brian Michael Good

"Eighty percent of all suicides fail. What, are you crazy? Your free will is taken away. Your life becomes far worse than it is now. Your life is a total mess as a result of your decision."

— Brian Michael Good

"Your children are born with free will. You cannot control their free will without consequences. You are meant to be their guide. If you read your children stories about angels or stories of virtues from a suitable book for children until the age of reasoning, they will learn many important life lessons that will help reinforce good behavior in your children as they mature. Positive reinforcement works far better than any form of discipline that causes excessive fear or anxiety in your child's development."

— Brian Michael Good

"Train yourself to think these thoughts, "I have free will. It is my choice." I suggest that if put a new plan into action and stay with this new attitude about how you might choose to view and live your life; you will positively have more happy moments than ever before in your lifetime."

— Brian Michael Good

"You are born with free will; you can give up or try to live."

— Brian Michael Good

"We all have free will that allows us to move forward by overcoming our self-pity. No one can defeat you. You can only defeat yourself. And that is a choice."

— Brian Michael Good

"Hoping for an entitlement is not what President Franklin Delano Roosevelt meant during his "Four Freedoms Speech" in his State of the Union Address on January 6, 1941: "The freedom of speech, the freedom of worship, the freedom from want, and the freedom from fear." "Freedom from want," means you have the responsibility to provide for your own needs and the free will to pursue the occupation of your choice."

— Brian Michael Good

"Proper training in self-defense can help our children learn self-control of their free will, allowing each of them to develop the self-confidence to walk away from other types of aggression knowing that the best form of self-defense comes from knowing that no one can defeat you. You can only defeat yourself."

— Brian Michael Good

"There are visual stimuli influencing your thoughts as to what happiness should be. A form of mind control. Happiness comes from owning your free will by controlling your thoughts with realistic expectations."

— Brian Michael Good

"Your children are born with free will. You cannot control their free will without consequences. You are meant to be their guides."

— Brian Michael Good

Generosity

"I am fortunate to live in a country where people believe in giving others a second chance."

— Brian Michael Good

"The Creator does not value money but Creator does care where your money came from and what you did with your money as you earned and spent it. It is what you do with your money for people of need."

— Brian Michael Good

"Authority, control, and wealth come with great responsibility. The Creator expects major shareholders, management and business owners to pay honest wages for an honest day's work. Greed does not give you any reward in the afterlife. You have already taken more than your fair share."

— Brian Michael Good

"Luxuries are not a necessity and someday we will realize that the money spent on luxuries could have greatly influenced most of the world's problems."

— Brian Michael Good

"How can the Creator justify retention of wealth when seventeen thousand children a day are dying of hunger? Over four hundred million go hungry on a daily basis, seven hundred and fifty million people do not have access to clean water, 1.2 billion people do not have access to electricity, 2.5 billion people lack adequate sanitation, and billions of people live without affordable housing? "

— Brian Michael Good

Gossip

"News always turns into gossip and gossip always turns into news. Only if you repeat it. It is a choice."

— Brian Michael Good

"The difference between gossip and news heard or seen in social media is getting harder to distinguish between what is true or not true. Best not to repeat what you hear or see even if it is verified. Then ask yourself whether you may be judging that person the same way they may be judged when you share the gossip or news."

— Brian Michael Good

"Rumors, hearsay and gossip are a one-sided story, a distortion of information because every time you gossip something in the story changes. This can cause misunderstandings, which can be a two-way street. When you spread rumors with gossip, it can affect how your peers view you. No one will ever trust you and thus you will not invite true friendships."

— Brian Michael Good

"Avoid gossip, bullying, rumors, hearsay, hazing, harassment, shaming, shunning, and slurs"

— Brian Michael Good

"The truth about gossip is the misinformation that is created can influence a teenager or anyone else' decision to die by suicide. Gossip can kill someone emotionally, mentally, physically and spiritually"

— Brian Michael Good

"If you participate in the gossip, you will be part of the chain of gossip that caused another person to repeat it after you. You may not know that the gossip that you participated in is spreading like fire. You may never know how far your gossip has traveled. If the gossip doesn't start in the first place or if you decide not to participate by refusing to listen to gossip; then the wildfire won't grow rapidly and the firefighters called the peacemakers don't need to called into action to put out the flames"

— Brian Michael Good

"You may not believe you will pay for your gossip. You might not even know that you need to be reflective. Everyone that participates in the gossip is at fault. If you gossip about someone then you may be judged by the Creator. The Creator considers the weak to be his special children even if they are adults. If you gossip over and over again you do not have the Creator in your heart and you just don't get it! You may be surrendering your soul."

— Brian Michael Good

Gratitude

"I spent three months in rehab and the next eight months at a homeless shelter in Cambridge, Massachusetts. That is when I realized that I had not appreciated how much I had before I attempted suicide."

— Brian Michael Good

"Everything we take for granted is a gift; most of us only realize its value upon its loss."

— Brian Michael Good

"Without the help of strangers, my recovery from my cancer and suicide attempt would have been quite difficult."

— Brian Michael Good

"There is no such thing as luck; everything good we experience in our lives is a gift and a blessing."

— Brian Michael Good

"You must find a way to live well even if you did not get the proper guidance from your parents, because you are the one who is responsible for your own life and the decisions you make. It is your choice."

— Brian Michael Good

"There is no such thing as luck, everything we take for granted is a gift and a blessing, and most of us only realize its value upon its loss."

— Brian Michael Good

"Appreciate what the Creator gave you by using what you have been given to the best of your ability."

— Brian Michael Good

Guidance

"You must find a way to live well even if you don't get the proper guidance from your parents because you are the one who is responsible for your own life and the decisions you make."

— Brian Michael Good

"A closed mind is like a parachute malfunction, a mind like a parachute only works if it is fully open."

— Brian Michael Good

"A human being is not what you are but who you can become if you choose to awaken to a greater reality. Most of us never attempt to grasp this."

— Brian Michael Good

"It is part of our human nature to question what we know and what we don't know."

— Brian Michael Good

"Each individual should focus on their own personal spiritual life; be aware that you may be surrendering your soul in your judgment or treatment of others."

— Brian Michael Good

"It may take you a lifetime to figure which direction you are headed but it might because when you were young you were never given a track to run on."

— Brian Michael Good

"Ninety percent of us exist, ten percent of us live. Choose to live well. Choose to live life to the fullest. Most of all, we should all do our Best to Live."

— Brian Michael Good

"In any good marriage, a woman's voice is equal to man's voice. The same should be true in our open society. Yes, women count as much as men. They count even more than men do, if you consider that women can do what men have considered to be "their domain" of feats, work, sports, business accomplishments, and bearing children. You have to admit Women are equal to men."

— Brian Michael Good

"We should not commercially hunt, allow testing, or separate any mammal from their family or social unit. Many mammals have similar emotional characteristics as humans. Who is to say they do not have souls, when many people believe that, their cat or dog will go to heaven. Just because we believe that human beings are the highest part of Creator's (God's) creation, does not make it so.

We have yet to explore the universe where there are estimated to be billions of Earth like planets. We might discover truths that would be inconceivable within our present day reality. Just because we have always hunted does not make it right to instill fear in the mammal we hunt.

Except for providing food for your family, thou shall not kill might pertain to many mammals of the animal kingdom."

— Brian Michael Good

"We must stop the present day slow genocide of Native Americans and their culture. Why are we still doing this? We are a Christian Nation… We need to be a Spiritual Nation.

There is little difference from what the settlers and the USA government (a Christian nation) did to the Native Americans and what the Catholic Church did during the Roman Catholic Inquisition. The Catholic Church had a history of collecting property and wealth from the dead after killing and torturing millions of Christians and Jews during the hundreds of years of the Roman Catholic Inquisition.

Over 500 treaties made with American Indian tribes were broken when it was to the United States government's advantage. The USA government helps its citizens in their recovery from national disasters. Yet, the present day genocide continues when Teen Suicide on American Indian reservations is almost three times the national rate, radiation from a nuclear dump threatens the Navajo/Hopi water supply, poor nutrition for many Native Americans has persisted for decades, and Apache sacred land was recently given to a copper company when a provision was approved by Congress."

— Brian Michael Good

93

Happiness

"You are in the center of your happiness when you pursue your passion."

— Brian Michael Good

"Be a lifeline for someone who needs your support. We will be undefeated in our pursuit of happiness. Be part of a Life Squad and find someone who needs a friend to lean on."

— Brian Michael Good

"How you manage your expectations is the secret to happiness and finding peace in your life."

— Brian Michael Good

"Peace and happiness are renewed for those who seek it."

— Brian Michael Good

"Accepting yourself the way you are is the secret to happiness and finding peace in your life."

— Brian Michael Good

"For many of us, it takes decades to realize that happiness comes from within us."

— Brian Michael Good

"Happiness is how our conscious thoughts react in harmony with the external sources and stimuli in our world."

— Brian Michael Good

"I realized that money gave me temporary happiness. As I matured to an adult, I began not to value money when my inability to sustain a consistent income became my new, but hopefully not permanent, reality."

— Brian Michael Good

"Now you know that life's happiness is all about your decision on how you react. It is never too late to take this road with thorns called life to where you want to be at. We are all human, be comfortable with this fact."

— Brian Michael Good

"Break the cycle. Create your own world of good and happiness."

— Brian Michael Good

"Choose to begin to change one day at a time, tiny steps where you position yourself in a steady motion of happiness and tranquility instead of allowing yourself to be hashed around beyond your control."

— Brian Michael Good

"There are visual stimuli influencing your thoughts as to what happiness should be. A form of mind control. Happiness comes from owning your free will by controlling your thoughts with realistic expectations."

— Brian Michael Good

"Elements Found in Happiness — Life, Free will, "Your soul – "your very essence", Dominion over other species, Sustenance, Shelter, Hope, Gratification, Love, Friendship, Creativity, Passion, and Destiny."

— Brian Michael Good

"The happiest moments that unite us as humans are when we enjoy music, dance, friends, family, and the birth of a child."

— Brian Michael Good

Hatred

"We are all exposed to the harsh realities of life. There is always going to be someone or a group of people who don't like you."

— Brian Michael Good

"Forgiving is not forgetting; it's actually remembering by not becoming an abuser; by using your free will not to hit back with anger, hatred, or revenge. It's an opportunity for a new beginning, a second chance, a learning experience by not allowing anyone to hurt or abuse you again."

— Brian Michael Good

Healing

"I have come to realize that without the engine; the body, getting a tune-up; the driver, the mind, cannot get where it wants to go in life very well. A healthy mind begins with a healthy body and vice versa."

— Brian Michael Good

"Sticks and stones may break your bones but you will decide if the words and names will ever hurt you. No one can defeat you. You can only defeat yourself. That is a choice."

— Brian Michael Good

"No one can defeat you. You can only defeat yourself. No one can truly save you. You must save yourself."

— Brian Michael Good

Health

"I do not drink liquor or beer on a regular basis and I no longer smoke cigarettes; the benefits go beyond my physical heath for my refrigerator and shelves and my life have an abundance of food that is now affordable."

— Brian Michael Good

"Some of us will experience some form of mental illness in their lifetime… I rather have depression that can be treated with a pill and my free will to conquer it; than have a physical illness that results in my demise because no matter what I did I could not conquer it."

— Brian Michael Good

"Think about a car not having ample petro/gas to start the engine, as the body not getting the proper nutrition, preventing the driver from arriving at their desired destination, an engaged mind likewise cannot develop the knowledge base of life skills that will be needed to achieve upward mobility."

— Brian Michael Good

"I have come to realize that without the engine; the body, getting a tune-up; the driver, the mind, cannot get where it wants to go in life very well. A healthy mind begins with a healthy body and vice versa."

— Brian Michael Good

"A person who is a little bit insane may be saner than someone who is completely sane. A little bit of insanity gives a person a better perspective on what the difference is between perception and reality."

— Brian Michael Good

"The clock's ticking... The longer you wait to change your life the harder it becomes to implement change. Sixty years old is mid-life if you consider that a healthy person with modern medical care might live to one hundred twenty. So what are you waiting for?"

— Brian Michael Good

"Everyone deserves a "Me" day without any guilt or regret... Relax and enjoy a day off."

— Brian Michael Good

Honor

"Originality is as RARE as finding an honest person. So many people on social media never give the author credit for use of their quote."

— Brian Michael Good

"Do not steal anything in any way."

— Brian Michael Good

"Integrity and honor should be part of every fabric of your beliefs."

— Brian Michael Good

"There is no honor in any killing. No family has the right to an "honor killing" when they kill a female relative."

— Brian Michael Good

"Honesty is very rare in our world and it is hard to find it in social media. Maybe we should favorite, retweet, like or add a quote to our social media a quote on social media only when the author is given proper credit."

— Brian Michael Good

"Just because it may be easy to go to peer-to-peer network and pirate or download a movie, music, or program free of charge does not mean you are not stealing it. Just because it is easy to share or copy your friend's music does not mean you are not stealing it. You have free will. Everything is a choice."

— Brian Michael Good

Hope

"Hope should never be extinguished; hope like the flame of a torch should be transferred to another torch before it flickers out allowing your hope to burn brightly again."

— Brian Michael Good

"You may not fully recover but you can adapt. The next battle is often won by finding a new source of hope that will push you forward."

— Brian Michael Good

"Acceptance of your failure is not an excuse to give up on any situation but to temporary accept defeat in order to retreat when the battle is lost to live to fight the battle another day with a new plan of action that gives you hope that victory is still attainable. You may not fully recover but you can adapt. The next battle is often won by finding a new source of hope that will push you forward."

— Brian Michael Good

"A dream not yet realized offers far more benefits than the reality one faces when they give up hope."

— Brian Michael Good

"To travel with hope is more important than arriving at your destination."

— Brian Michael Good

"Never give up hope; for without hope; food, water, faith or beliefs will not be enough to nourish your body, mind and soul."

— Brian Michael Good

Humility

"It is difficult to be humble when you are recognized for your achievements. It is better to keep your achievements to yourself by staying under the radar and remain humble."

— Brian Michael Good

Inspiration

"You cannot rush inspiration, for inspiration comes from the body, mind, soul, and the cosmos."

— Brian Michael Good
